MEMORIES UNWOUND

RUBY DHAL

Dear Mum

I know no matter where I go
I will never find another you.

I love you.

To every single person who has been exhausted in love but didn't let it break them.

PREFACE

'Memories Unwound' is a collection of free verse poems and prose that tap into the thoughts, feelings and experiences of the author. Each piece aims to go beyond just words and reveal an emotion; love, pain and happiness and by the end of it the prospect of attaining solace. The author uses 'memories' as a title to emphasise that it is universally relatable – as readers should find at least one (or more) piece(s) that remind them of a previous experience they have had or an emotion they have felt, hence becoming a 'memory' that is unwound in this book.

Each piece aims to uncover sentiments that fabricate our very being, and by the end of the book readers are shown the possibility of hope, redemption, closing 'old chapters' and moving on to make new memories.

1. EXPERIENCE

2. LOVE

3. HURT

4. HEAL

- Time to unwind.

A memory never felt like just a visual image of a time that has long passed, consisting of people, places and things that have long vanished. For me, memories were the sort of entities that took me back to good things, good people and good places. They made me smile and laugh through my tears, they warmed my insides with familiarity, they made me feel giddy, nostalgic and euphoric. And often, they burned my soul and paced the beating of my heart. But I always welcomed them open-armed, every single time. I ushered them in and placed them – and everything that they represented – on a stage in the centre of my mind where they received all my attention. And when they decided to leave, I escorted them with pride and honour until next time. Until the next time they came knocking, ready to unwind, bringing with them a hurricane of emotions. Until next time,

I said.

Until next time.

EXPERIENCE

My mother was the epitome of grace.

She had skin the colour of rain-washed sand and thick boisterous hair the colour of the night. It was long and hefty and wrapped itself around her tender frame like rich twine. Her smile could kill a thousand hurricanes and change the course of the wind. Her eyes, tiny hazel almonds that shone more than the brightest star in the sky, told stories of an era she had left behind. 'But my heart knows of no colour', her gaze always said. My heart knows of no colour. And tonight, I look at my face, her face, and I ask myself,

So, why does yours?

Fall,

Fall as many times as you can
but remember –

you will rise again.

It took me quite
a while to
figure out that
the other side of
truth isn't as
beautiful

as it seems.

Yes, you are the product of your experiences, of everything that life has thrown your way. Of every rise and every fall. But you are also the product of the choices that you make. Of blaming the world or choosing to take responsibility, of losing hope or choosing to give yourself another chance, of remaining broken or choosing to rise again.

The whole world
is going crazy,
and here I am
thinking that it was
just me.

Change is what
we all seek
yet it is
a door that
nobody wants
to open.

She didn't belong on earth. She belonged on a throne that rested on a silver-lined cloud overhead, where self-love and affection were taught and people were respected, where greed was nowhere to be found and love was all that they ever worshipped.

I can't lie and say that
I learned from my past
and nothing hurts me
anymore,
because
I'm still human,
I still get hurt
my emotions are strong
and my feelings haven't
changed,

– just those who have power over them have.

Sometimes I look at you and wonder where you get all this strength from, and I can't help but praise, your ability to endure the toughest storm and never crumble, your will, that allows you to love unconditionally and irrevocably, and your heart that appears as vast as the universe and as deep as the ocean. I gasp at all of this and everything else that fabricates your soul, and I am in awe, believe me,

I am in awe.

You are all
the hopes,
dreams,
fears
and anxieties

That keep you up
at night.

The colour of my skin
does not define my beauty,

It is the colour
of my soul
that you should be

more concerned with.

She never understood
the world
and its perverse ways
and the world
never understood
her innocence.

I will believe you when you show me where
he is. He, who can love me, strengthen me
and build me up not to tear me back down.
He, who will hear me, comfort me and tell me
that I am complete in myself, that I always
have been. Show me where he is, for right
now he only exists in the deepest corners of
my mind.

(the one)

Listen carefully to
the soft whispers
of your soul,
they will tell you
about all the
blooming secrets
hidden beneath
these bones.

(secrets speak too)

You won't see the stars in my eyes.
You'll see remnants
of battles lost and won
and a tarnished moon inside,
you'll see what it's like
to sail through life's
chaotic debacle and
remain uninjured,
you'll see speckles of dust
and lots of rain but you won't
see the stars,

For the stars are what you need
to wish upon
to get a glimpse of
all of this.

It kills to know
the world you see
is not
as beautiful
as you thought it was,
but it kills
even more
when you falsely believe
that you cannot
make it that way.

I can't cite powerful stories about how the past teaches you in such a way that you become whole again. But what I can say is this; sometimes the past is a teacher and sometimes regret is. And the biggest thing both can teach you is not how to heal, for that is a necessary bi-product of time itself. What both can teach you is that if you want to remain whole, then you must remove yourself from those who will inevitably break you.

– you are my angel and nothing less.

'What can I do for you?' I ask.
I am nothing but a tarnished soul
wrapped around heartache,
broken, healing and changing.

'What can I give you?' I ask.
I am nothing
but an empty vessel
held aloft on the heat of lost love,
moving, mending and racing.

'I am no good to you.' I say.
I am no good to you.

I learnt not too long ago that people
hear what they want to.
That's why when I said I'm happy,
they heard I'm sad,
when I said I'm sad
they heard I'm broken,
when I said I'm broken
they heard I need help
and when I asked for help –

They heard nothing at all.

You aren't just skin and bone or what meets the eye. You are all your hopes, lost and found, your dreams, incomplete and those that survive, those fears that keep you up at night, the tears, happy and sad, that won't leave your side. You are heart and soul and everything that lies in between. You are you, beautiful, tarnished you. The you that everyone can see but no one has truly seen.

It is in the end
that we find
a new beginning,

It was in heartbreak
that I found you.

She was sunshine.
Not the kind you took
shelter from,
the kind you
soaked your soul in.

Have you ever felt like a drifter?
A piercing hole,
a heartache wrapped
in crisp yellow paper
knocking on someone
else's door?

Have you ever thought
that perhaps you are
the answer to someone's
prayer, the solace to
someone's pain,
a home to another's
lost heart,
the door to their soul?

Have you ever thought?

In every today,
an essence of yesterday

– still lingers.

Here's what it is. We can go through so many hardships in life and remain positive, happy, still be unbreakable, unscathed. When really, it will take just one bad experience to turn our whole world around, to burn everything that we had to live for. And that's what just doesn't make sense about us.

Kind souls aren't easily recognisable. They're the smudged faces in tumbling crowds, the quiet voices that we try to down, the righteous morals easily overthrown, the blooming hearts that we don't listen to. These souls think, wander and soar. They fight, and fight and fight, but we fail to acknowledge. They're warm rays of sunlight peeking through thin gaps in our stone-structured lives. But that's the issue, for it is the kind of sunlight that is so easily covered by the storm.

Oh, how beautifully
tragic
it is to watch
the silent sobbing
of your heart,
it is like droplets of light
falling from a universe
hidden within your eyes,
it is like the stars are
raining down
from a painfully dark sky.

She was a star.

The kind that
didn't go a day
without burning
so that he
didn't go a day
without light.

Believe me when I say this. Everyone is fighting a battle of their own, facing their own personal struggles and going through different kinds of pain. It takes just a second to notice. So, if you looked carefully and paid enough attention, you'd see that you're not alone. You never were.

Never search for validation
in other people's eyes,

your validation comes
from within,

your worth comes
from within.

Women like her don't come by often. They're not easy to find. They grow from the depths of chaos where broken hopes and incomplete dreams are found, where people are empty and emotions bare. But somehow, women like her boom and burst through the moss and soar like butterflies. The kind of butterflies that were not made to be tamed.

When life
starts to feel as quiet as
a steady ocean, I can't help
but wonder
whether this is the calm

– before the storm.

You are a diamond. A diamond dressed in sprigs and dirt which fail to tarnish it. A diamond made to cure crippled hearts and broken souls. A diamond that bleeds starlight and reflects the universe in her eyes. You are a diamond, and don't you forget it.

LOVE

Let's go half and half, you and I. You can be the sun, I'll be the moon. You can be the earth, I'll be the air. You're the sky, I'm the ground. You're water, I'm fire. You're hot, I'm cold. You're here, I'm there. You're up, I'm down. You're happy, I'm sad. You're tears, I'm joy. You're love, I'm hate. You smile, I cry. You're fast, I'm slow. You're everything to me, and I'll be every-thing to you. And in the end, you'll be the wind that swept me off my feet, and I,

The one who flew.

When your mind stands still
and your heart does all the talking,
you know you are in love –

You have fallen in it too.

He loved me from the
deepest core of his being,
until love exhaled
from his every breath,
seeped from
his every pore
and soaked his face
with every tear,
it was nothing but
love, love, love.

And when I finally
felt it too,
I let him
hand me his soul
and peel off
every single layer
of mine.

– I am bleeding galaxies for you tonight.

You are the earth
beneath the footprints
of this bare heart,
the veins that are etched
under these thin wrists,
the love that seeps through
these wary bones.

You are within me.

Here, I give you my heart.

But be kind to it,
be gentle.
It as seen many
harsh winters
battled storms
fought demons
throbbed under
the wind
chased the setting sun,
but it is yours
to keep now.

So, be kind to it,
be gentle.

Our level of understanding
is different,
it takes just one smile,
one breath,
one blink
and it is like we've had
a world of conversations
together.

And you know too
that no matter where your heart goes,
across the horizon,
past the silver-lined moon
washed away in the sea
and through each changing
season,
it will always find its way
back to me.

Beauty is contingent,
fall in love with a soul.

(eternal love)

You are love. Honest, patient and kind. A love that loiters, a love that breathes. You take root in dry soil, you settle in empty cracked hearts. Your beauty is infinite, your essence pure. You're not defined by those who couldn't understand you, by those who didn't have the strength to take you forward. In all your beautiful tarnished splendour, darling, you are love.

And sometimes,
I can't help
but wonder,
does love know
what it's like
to love someone?
Does it?

Tonight,
the moon throbs brightly,
I whisper to it
and in turn
it whispers to you.

(moonlit conversations)

I didn't want
a heart for a heart,
I wanted
a fear for a fear
a scar for a scar
a dream for a dream

– a soul for a soul.

Your voice sounds familiar,
it is a soft echo
a sweet lullaby
a soothing hymn
that has played in my mind
over and over again.

A pretty face didn't attract her. She desired a man with a burning intellect. The kind who challenged her and made her guess, think and imagine. The kind who was puzzling, exciting and wondrous at the same time. The kind who warmed her mind and made her heart nervous. The kind who pulled her towards him and constantly kept her on her toes in speculation of just what this man was really about.

It's only when
you find someone
worth dreaming with
that you realise
all those years
they were worth
dreaming for.

Don't tell me.
Don't tell me your skin
is the limit when
I can see footprints
on your heart.

Take me to the other side of love,

The side that drifts and wanders,
the side that heals all wounds,
the side that understands,
cares and worries,
the side that heals two
broken pieces together.

Take me to the other side of love,

The side where there is you and me,
our hopes and dreams
your wishes
my fears
our present years,
the side where your eyes shine
and my heart feels faint,
where your smile pierces
through my soul and I finally
realise that this is
where it all begins.

Take me to the other side.

Your eyes tell me
a thousand stories
a thousand times –

in a split second.

And before our hearts meet
our broken pieces
will find each other,
connecting
uniting
merging as one,
and setting
our souls on fire.

You and I
You and I
You and I,

It's the only world
that I have
ever known.

I once dreamt
about a patient love,
kind to the core
and pure in its depth,
one that healed all
that was sore within me.

I woke up and found you.

Wherever I go,
and the wind
starts throbbing
and the sun loses its glow,
I know you are there too.

(you never leave my side)

I promise,
hurtle across
the ocean and
I promise to
catch you if you fall.

Even your heart knows
that you cannot find
the same love that I wore
like poetry
across my sleeve
for you.

I only know silence
that carves out words
unspoken, but heard,
unexpressed, but felt.

It's only in such silence
that I can hear you
speaking to me.

(silent conversations)

Love is giving him
half a glass of water
in the desert, when
half a glass of water
is all you have.

Do I lay away in your dreams as well?

Like a tender wound
a soft whisper
a steady hum
waiting, waiting, waiting,
to be held all night
under the fading moon.

I write about everything,
but mostly I write about
all that was unsaid,
inked words
that hung loosely
between us,
pressing our breaths,
making their way
to our throats,
entwining themselves
around our limbs
until they held
our hearts captive.

Those words spoke volumes.

I have been told
I feel too much
care too much
give too much,
but this is the only
manner of loving
that I have ever known.

On nights like this,
my soul whispers
to the wind to carry you
back to me.

(come home)

It was among the loose words
etched on crinkled paper,
tiny poems from me to you,
from you to me
in which we lost ourselves,
and I haven't found myself
since.

He is the reason for
all the love poems
I didn't have the strength
to complete.

One day, you will be
with someone
who will have the strength
to love you just as much
as you love them.

Do you know what it's like to love someone? Let me explain. You take your desires, wishes, dreams, hopes, fears and happiness, put them all in an empty jar and hand it over to them. You don't ask any questions and you don't tell them what to do with it. You just trust them enough to give it all away.

Think twice before you shatter,
for you are a beautiful white dove
silver-lined with splendour,
kindled with love
and needled together

with pieces of my heart.

Don't say I've forgotten you.

I keep you close to me
every single day,
like poetry scrawled
on empty palms,
and when it washes off
I keep you alive
in the stories that
I write at night.

I haven't felt this departed from reality
in a long, long time.

I'm falling in love again,
all over again.

She isn't made for simple hello's, small talk, wary smiles, empty glances, flirting and infatuated moments. She's made for adventures, road trips and late night ice cream. She's made to see a star dazed sky and the falling sun with. She's made for quiet whispers in dim-lit movie theatres. She's made for beach walks and conversations that last until the early hours of dawn. She's made to experience silence that soothes your heart and music that fuels your soul. And she's made to do the one thing that you fear to do the most.

She's made to fall in love with.

– this love will be the end of me.

HURT

You will stop hurting, believe me. You will stop hurting the day you fall in love with someone who has the same meaning of love as you.

(you will stop hurting)

I guess I truly lost you
when I realised that
all I had were
stolen moments
that never
really belonged to me,
and when I saw
that those moments
weren't mine to keep,
I also knew
neither were you.

I know you would trade
a thousand tomorrows and
a thousand todays
to go back to
just one yesterday.

I've stopped.
I've stopped giving
parts of myself
to help heal others,
because in the end
when they start to
feel complete again,
I am the one that
ends up with
all the missing pieces.

These days I'm running out of things
to write about, and I don't know
if it's because I'm losing words
or because I'm losing you.

Hand me a shovel,
I will dig my way through
this sorrow
just like you
dug your way
through every heart
that fell for you.

I know, one day I'll
stop pretending like
nothing bothers me
and unveil myself
to the world,
but I fear,
I fear for those
who will witness
the brutal rawness
of my bare soul.

Believe me,
you're worth it but
he's not
for giving up
on you.

I don't know what else to say,
but just know that days like this
will pass too.

And in the end
we'll spend the rest of
our lives
searching in the arms
of others
for the kind of comfort
that we could only find
in our first love.

Believe me. You're not the only one who's broken. Because if you looked close enough, you'll only find remnants of scars and wounds from past experiences that make up quarters and halves where there would have otherwise been wholes.

Sometimes my heart
starts burning
with thoughts
of you.

Do you remember,

That night where our hearts
spoke in poetry
and our lips sealed truths
for years to come?

Do you remember,

That night where you
tore away our language
and everything inside me
went numb?

We spend our nights
dreaming about the right things,
we spend our days doing
the wrong ones.

The silver-lined moon
doesn't look as beautiful
as it used to,
it's crazy how you took
it all with you,
the beauty
the light
the spark
of life.

(lost love)

Evenings are filled
with the comfort of
your words
soft against my skin,
mornings are filled
with heavy air
resulting from the
emptiness
that those words bring.

Let's just pretend
nothing went wrong,
you never left
the sky never turned grey,
the stars never lost their glow
the sun never hid away,
the birds kept singing
and we breezed through life
each day,
but
what happened?

Things never stayed the same,
and somehow it all ended and
no one was really to blame.

And that,
my love
is the tragedy
of falling
so effortlessly
for the wrong person

once again.

Honey, you need to stop
searching for happiness
in all the wrong places.

Every time I get hurt
a part of me dies,
it's almost as if
bit by bit
piece by piece
I'm losing myself.

I know
I'll find my way
back around again,
but right now
I just need time.

Dear queen,
you may be broken but

– you are still worthy.

I have moved on.
but tucked away in
a little corner of my mind
are your memories,
they are mine to keep
even if you weren't.

(what's mine stays with me)

On rare occasions like today
I end up scrawling
the letters of your name
on my wrist,
only to scrub them
off later,
in hope that
it will erase you
from my heart too.

We let them rest
on a throne
settled in the centre
of our heart
and then we wonder
why they have
this much power
over us.

He never understood
that she wasn't made
for games –

She was made for love.

It took getting to know
every single part of me
to realise that
you weren't there

anymore.

Life had its way
of showing me
what mattered and
what didn't,
who mattered and
who didn't,
but
if only it could have
shown me
when love was real
and when it wasn't.

Tell me one thing.

Being a good girl
never did you any good,
did it?

The world is too harsh sometimes,
it screams,
it shouts,
it tells me things that
I refuse to hear.

The world is too cruel sometimes,
it pulls you
it snatches
knowing that I'll only survive
if you're somewhere near.

I wish you had the strength
to fight for her
because if you did
you wouldn't have just
won her,
you would've won
your whole world.

Sometimes,
I think our hearts just have
minds of their own.

I have given this heart
so many excuses
but never the truth,
that it wasn't me who left
it was you.

Sometimes,
a thought is all it takes
to break down
every bit of courage
you had been building up.

One thing
heartbreak teaches you
is that –

Eyes can lie too.

I pray that you are showered with serenity all around. I pray that your smile never leaves you. And I pray, and pray, and pray. For it to finally rain love on you. The kind of love that will drench your soul but not your cheeks. The kind of love that will make your heart and not your throat skip a beat. The kind of love that is pure. The kind of love that is warm. The kind of love that throbs happiness in all its being. The kind of love that we both knew I always deserved.

Sometimes you love them
in such a way that
you feel
incomplete
with them and
incomplete
without them.

I wish I said 'no' on many occasions I responded with a 'yes' in. I could have saved so much of myself that my yes's gave away.

– we fought until we had nothing left to fight for.

I can't keep repairing
everything that you damaged,
all the pieces
laying by my feet,
I can't keep fixing
what you broke,
I can't keep cleaning up
all the mess
that you made.

That night
he told me about
all the stories that
he left behind
and I told him about
all the stories
that left me.

Don't feel sorry
for hurting
for tearing
for bruising
the way you do.

You're only human
darling,
you're only human.

I guess
we're just all
contained by
broken promises
and false dreams
mixed with a lot of love
and a heart
that just wants
to scream.

Loving scares me,
because you can take
every single part
of another person
as if it belongs to you
and keep it close to your heart,
yet still feel empty.

(this is why loving scares me)

Sometimes my heart is
too full of emotions
and sometimes
it feels too empty,
I guess just like me
my heart, too,
knows of no boundaries.

And when you see yourself
starting to crack,
thin brown lines crawling their way
through to your heart,
hold yourself together
as tight as you can,
don't let those pieces go
because if you do
you'll lose parts of yourself
that you will never find again.

And I will spend the rest of this life
waiting
to know what
it's like to be
on the other side
of love.

HEAL

I write to unite all
that has crumbled
inside me,

– I write to heal.

Dance like a butterfly, soar like the wind. Battle those demons of love that threaten to perish you, that threaten to kill. They tell you that you're not worthy. Smile at them. For you are a beauty in disguise. Kill them with kindness, kill them with love. And don't ever forget that you are enough.

(you always have been)

In the end
no one can understand you
until you understand yourself,
and no one can love you
until you love yourself.

Some women dream of a world
where their wings aren't confined
and nor is their heart,
she was the kind of woman
who made all their dreams
come true.

Give me everything
you were scared to give her,
I promise
I will keep it safe,
I promise
I will take care of you.

– kill the fear, not the feeling.

I've seen the sun cry as you make yourself whole again, as you mould together fragments of broken wars; a tired heart and limbs torn. Cleaning up the mess as you go, making sure you don't leave a speckle of dirt in your wake.

(I've seen it all)

I'm sorry
I can't keep pretending
that I need you,
because I know
I know,
that I will make it –

with or without you.

Darling,
you need to understand that
all the solace you seek
can only be found within.

(Letter to you)

Dear you,
I'm ready to tell you this,
so, listen.
I need you to stop worrying about me
I'm finally okay.
I know
we both know,
I endured a storm that toppled
my whole world over and
made my heart come undone,
I was shattered,
broken.
I agree.
But I'm so much better now,
time mended every single wound
and love,
love healed me in ways
unimaginable,
and happiness finally
laced itself around me
and picked me up
up for good.

I'm ready to tell you this,
it's time to say goodbye.
Because I'm finally okay
I really am.

Crippled wings,
aching bones,
wounded soul
but her halo
continues to glow.

It feels as though I've gone through hell
and soared fiercely, untamed, unscathed.

It feels as though I've stumbled and
descended and pulled myself upright,
feeling stronger, feeling reborn.

'What do you want from me?' He asks.

I want you,
all of you.
including every scar
every wound
every pain
every worry
every fear
every insecurity –

I want it all.

I've stopped.
I've stopped searching
for light in other people's
hearts,
I learned not too long ago
how self-destructive it is
to search for
a gleaming sun that
can only dwell within.

Sometimes
saying sorry isn't enough
to stitch together
everything that has torn inside,
and sometimes
a sorry that has the power
to heal you
just never comes.

Being with someone
you love
and being with someone
that loves you
isn't always
the same thing.

She wasn't from here. Her eyes were chalky pearls and her skin glittered. The blood that coursed through her veins was deep blue velvet. And sure, she was made of stardust like the rest of us, but her scent was magical, the sort of magic that you wished upon a shooting star. And that is why, she was magnificent.

Don't hide behind your layers,
don't etch yourself clean,
be you,
the beautiful organic you
the you
that hid for so long,
the you
no one has ever seen.

I can't keep pretending that
that I didn't break
I didn't hurt
and I didn't weep in the way
you felt I should have,
but I also can't keep pretending
that I didn't rise
I didn't heal
I didn't soar
in ways you never
thought I would have.

Mend those torn limbs of love that fear to bruise again, that fear to shatter. Let the wind mop away any tears, let it murmur sweet melodies to your soul, let it heal you in ways you never knew. For tomorrow is a new day, a new beginning. An essence of hope lingers around the corner and it whispers to you, there is a way.

(there is a way)

Distance yourself
from everything that
upsets you,
shakes you and
harms your mind
in ways it shouldn't.

Distance yourself
from everything toxic.

The most comforting silence
is shared with your soul mate,
it is ironic
how I found that comfort
only with myself,
but I know now that
I am my own soul mate.

I don't hurt as much as I used to before,
not because time heals all wounds –

but because love does.

I've stood standstill, watching leaves change colour and seasons grow, witnessing life flow like a river; slow and steady and sometimes stunned with just one question lingering in my mind. The day he walked into my life, like a crisp wind on a dry summer afternoon, I felt that I would get all my answers. 'Why do you love me?', I asked him, with just one answer throbbing in my mind. I hoped that it would leave his mouth and tingle in my ears. But, just like the rest, he answered incorrectly, blaming the glittering of my skin and the colour of my eyes as the causes of his affection. I stood up and left without another word. And I set off in search once again, through the fluctuating pattern of life to find someone, anyone, who would tell me why I was worth loving. Someone who was strong enough to admit that it wasn't my outer layers that pulled him, but what had always been within.

(my soul)

You will heal.
You will heal.
You will heal.

The darkness and I go
a long way back,
because every time
I seem to lose myself,
it pierces through
my soul to let the
moon back in again –

And the light follows.

Paint the grey sky,

Orange, crimson and blue,
just like the first ray of sunlight
that hues your world
with warmth.

Paint it as you wish,

For as long as you believe
that it was meant this way
just for you.

You heard my cries for help but you never heard the self-healing songs that dwelled within me. You only chose to hear what you wanted to, because in the end, you thought that you were my remedy, when really, I myself was the only cure to it all.

Comfort your heart, and
comfort your spirit
then watch how they both
comfort you.

How easy would life be
if we could speak
with one another
in silence
instead of words?

How simple would life be?

For even our anger
would be
quiet and calm,
and for once
even our tears
would truly be felt.

Let me take a shower. Let me wash away dirt that my past experiences left behind. Let me clean eyes that have seen too much. Let me wipe away this heart that has felt too much. Let me soak these tired fingertips. Let me dust away any filth. Let me scrub and swab every part of myself that has a lingering essence of yesterday. And let me start again. All over again.

The innate power of words
is unfathomable to some,
and that is why they fail
to discern that,
often,
words touch them
before people do.

I'm shredding off
all my layers tonight,
every layer up until
the very last.

And I'm hoping
that it will be
the last of you too.

In this lifetime
I want to experience self-love,
the kind that strengthens,
revives and
holds me together,
the kind of love that
heals itself
mends itself
and cures itself of all scars
of all wounds,
the only kind of love that is
pure in all its depth and
crimson to the core.

This is the only love I am searching for.
This is the only love I wish to know.
This is the only love that I am worth.

(self-love)

And one day
she voyaged on
a new journey,
searching for
a once in a lifetime
kind of love,

– once again.

Days where
my mind feels heavy
  leads to nights
    where my soul
      gets
       set

        free.

Don't wait for love to heal what's broken. Teach yourself that it is okay. Whisper to your soul. Kindle your spirit. Comfort your heart. And when you finally feel complete, love will come, love will smile, love will praise and love will be there for you. But love won't do anything that you can't do for yourself.

You are sunshine,
and one day you
are going to light up
someone's world
in a way no one else
could before –

And don't you forget it.

Strength grew from her pores
and glistened
on her bare surface,
a thousand flecks
of stardust were
sprinkled like
gemstones
on her skin

– gleaming fearlessly for the world to see.

In loving you
I didn't know how far I strayed
until I was in the middle
of nowhere
and it was time
to find my way back home again.

(all alone)

(serenity)

It seems as though
it was just yesterday
that I came to you
leaving a
lifetime
of worries
behind.

I have felt pain and endured for too long. I have stumbled and fallen and risen once more. I'm stronger now than I've ever been, more in control. Fiercer. Sharper. Because when it all came tumbling down, life laced itself around me and made me whole again. And I became the person who could experience anything and never break, the person who was destined to take life's difficult journeys and soar through them. The person who felt, endured and wavered but never gave up.

The only person I was always meant to be.

Let me heal you.

Let me heal you
in a way no one ever has before,
I'll drink your tears
and kiss your scars
and I'll hold you so close that
you'll never
feel alone again.

I have never felt more content
in my life,
I have never felt more secure,
I guess that's what
it feels like
to heal completely,
I guess that's what it means
to be cured.

I love spending time
with people who
ease my soul
who make me feel light
on my feet,
people who clear my mind
and soothe my heart,
people who are
as true as love and
as real as the universe,
these are my kind of people.

(people who feel like home)

She did everything,
she smiled
she laughed and
she cried,
she was strong
with a will
to go on,
and when
nothing worked
she said goodbye

– and she moved on.

Someone once told me that I wasn't unique, that girls like me could be found anywhere. So, I started looking. I searched and searched, to the ends of the earth, I looked high and low, here and there, through every edge, corner and curve. But I couldn't do it. I couldn't find another me. And then I started to hurt, because I realised that if I couldn't find another me, then all those years, neither could you.

One day
someone will love you
the way you deserve
to be loved
and you won't have to

– fight for it.

I helped myself.

I wiped my own tears
put balm over fresh wounds
plastered parts of myself
that were still hurting,
gave myself some time
read books that soothed my heart
heard music that calmed my nerves
watched movies that made me smile,
bit by bit and piece by piece
I put myself back together again
and I gave myself a second chance,
because I knew that if I didn't
then no one else would.

It's time for forgiveness.

Forgive yourself.
Forgive, for your heart
breaking relentlessly.
Forgive, for refusing to mend.
Forgive, for weeping,
for hurting.
Forgive, for loving
those unworthy.
Forgive, for cursing
those scars that make you.
Forgive, for hating your mind,
your body and your soul.
Forgive, for being
so hard on yourself.
and finally,

Forgive, for taking this long
to forgive yourself.

WHO AM I

'Who am I?'

I am my mother's big brown eyes and the piercing gaze that settled within them. I am my father's workman hands; the rigid texture, the grease permanently etched on tired fingertips. I am my mother's slender frame and the heart that lay beneath. I am her smile, her tears and her lifelong dreams. I am my father's bottle up anxieties, his sweltering days and his tired nights. I am the reflection of fear they took with them to foreign land, a manifestation of the gamble they took on life. I am the fractional outburst of what resulted, an empty vessel, the only remnant of love laced around them, slowly coming undone.

ABOUT THE AUTHOR

Ruby Dhal is a poetess, writer and aspiring novelist currently residing in the UK. As a young child, Ruby used books as a form of escapism from painful experiences of the real world. As she grew older she realised that books were meant to take her closer to reality and brought her at one with her true self. Through reading and writing poetry, she discovered herself and walked on a new path through which she learned about self-love and revival, and she then sought out to do the same for others. Her passion for writing and revealing countless emotions for the world to share in has allowed Ruby to receive an endless amount of love and support from a generous social media following. Her first book was extremely well-received by her readers and it is for this reason that she wrote a second edition to allow her readers to once more take a journey through love and heartbreak with purpose of healing and discovering one's true depths. When Ruby isn't writing poetry, she is working on her first novel which is based on many true events that have taken place in her life. You can find Ruby on Instagram (@r.dhalwriter), Facebook (@r.dhalwriter) and Twitter (rdhalwriter).

ACKNOWLEDGEMENTS

To my mother. I know you're out there some-where watching me with a kind smile and that gleam in your big brown eyes that had the pow-er to melt even the stonehearted. And I want to thank you. I want to thank you for bringing me into this world and passing down all your values to me despite me being unfortunate enough not to have grown under your wing. I want to thank you for blessing me with your heart, although I've been told it is a little too soft sometimes, for blessing me with your eyes, they're beautiful – I've been told countless times – and for blessing me from wherever your throne is resting every single day. I love you and I always will.

To my father. Thank you for holding my hand when the love of your life left it. Thank you for teaching me everything from how to ride a bike, to how to stand up for myself and to the more valuable lessons of how to fight each bat-tle in my life. Thank you for teaching me about strength, resilience and kindness. And thank you for loving me unconditionally. You are the rea-son why I am this woman today.

To my brother. Thank you for being the biggest blessing in my life. You are and always will be my saviour, my angel, the one who believed in me when I didn't even believe in myself and the sole reason for why I dream. You took care of me, you loved me and you supported me. You are the anchor of my ship and you will always be the one person I look up to more than anything. Despite it all, we made it through together and isn't that a wonderful thing?